Backyard Books

Are You an Ant?

For the children and staff of the
Wandle Primary School, Wandsworth, England—J. A. and T. H.

KINGFISHER
Larousse Kingfisher Chambers Inc.
80 Maiden Lane
New York, New York 10038
www.kingfisherpub.com

First published in 2002

2 4 6 8 10 9 7 5 3 1

1TR/1201/TWP/GRS/150NYM

LIBRARY OF CONGRESS CATALOGING-IN-PUBLICATION DATA
Allen, Judy.
Are you an ant? / by Judy Allen;
illustrated by Tudor Humphries.—1st ed.
p. cm. – (Backyard books)
ISBN 0-7534-5365-7
1. Ants—Juvenile literature. [1. Ants.]
I. Humphries, Tudor, ill. II. Title.

QL568.F7 A45 2001
595.79'6–dc21   2001018664

Editor: Carron Brown
Series Designer: Jane Buckley

Printed in Singapore

Backyard Books

Are you an Ant?

Judy Allen and Tudor Humphries

KING*f*ISHER

NEW YORK

Are you an ant?

If you are,
your mother is a queen.

One hot summer day she went
on a mating flight with
thousands of others so that
she would be able to lay eggs.

Afterward she flew down to the ground. She knew she didn't need her wings anymore, so she took them off.

Then she dug herself a small room underground.

Now that she is in her room,
the queen begins to lay eggs.
You are in one of them.
Hatch out of the egg
as soon as you can.

You don't look like an ant yet.
You're a larva, and you're hungry.
There are eggs all over the place.
Eat some. It's all right; they won't mind.
They're only eggs.

Soon you must change into a pupa.
A pupa is a little like an egg, only
bigger. When you're ready, break out!

You look almost like an ant—
but you're white and soft.

Don't worry.
Slowly your skin will become hard
and black, and you'll look perfect.
There are a lot of others like you.
You are one of a big family.
You are a worker!

Work hard to build a nest. Dig
storage rooms and nurseries
and bedrooms and corridors.

10

It's all right; you don't
have to work alone. The
others will work with you.

You don't have
any voices, but you can talk to
each other by touching feelers.

11

Don't eat any more eggs.
Go out and hunt for food.
Seeds are nice. So are bugs
and wood lice. Springtails
are delicious, but hard to
catch because they jump.

Bite your prey and spray
it with acid from your tail.
Actually, you're not a very
good hunter. Look for
bugs that have been
stepped on. They're easy.

You may think there's easy food in kitchens, but be careful. There are crumbs and grains of sugar, which are nice. There are also people, and they're not so nice.

People don't like you in their homes. They may squash you. They may poison you. Or they may sweep the floor so you can't find anything to eat.

The best food is honeydew.
It comes from aphids.
Find a plant with aphids
feeding on it.

March up the stem
with the other workers.
Now stroke an aphid until
it gives you a drop of honeydew.

It's a little like
milking a cow, but you wouldn't
know about that—you're an ant.

Take care of your aphids.

Ladybugs eat aphids—
so look for ladybug eggs
and throw them away.

You must take food
back to the nest.

Some you can lift.

Some you can drag.

Some you can put in your second stomach. It's called a crop, and it's very useful for carrying spare food home.

Back at the nest,
there's plenty to do.
Feed the queen—
who is still laying eggs.
Feed the larvae—
who are still hatching.

Take care of
the eggs and larvae.
When it's cold, carry them
deep into the nest, where it's cozy.
When the sun warms the ground,
carry them up near the surface.

Oh—and don't forget to take
out the garbage.

Life isn't all food and work.
There's danger, too.
Birds and lizards and toads
think you are good
to eat.

Some birds
pick you up and push
you under their wings.
Why? Because the acid in your
body kills the ticks that bite
them and make them itch.
This is called anting.

Anting is nice for birds.
Anting is not nice for ants.

However, if your family looks a little

like this

or this

or this

you are not an ant.

You are...

25

...a human child.

You don't have
to take care of eggs
and larvae.

You don't have
to milk aphids.

You probably don't
have to march in a line
with a lot of others.

Don't worry—you can
do many things that
ants can't do.

Best of all, no bird is ever,
ever, EVER going to pick
you up in its beak and
stuff you under its wing.

29

Did You Know...

...the ants in this book are black garden ants, but there are about 10,000 different kinds of ants living all over the world.

...some grow their own food—South American leafcutter ants carry pieces of leaves home and chew them up to make compost for their fungus gardens.

...some are hunters—thousands of African driver ants march in long columns, eating any animal in their path if it doesn't escape in time!

...some collect seeds and fruits and honeydew—these ants leave a scent trail to guide their worker sisters to the food.

...some ants can sting, so be careful!